PHILIP GROSS &   ...1S

Philip Gross was born in 1952 in Delabole, Cornwall (beside the slate quarry). He grew up in Plymouth, studied English at Sussex University, and later trained as a librarian. He now lives in Bristol.

In 1981 he received a Gregory Award from the Society of Authors, and in 1982 won first prize in the Poetry Society's National Poetry Competition. His first radio play, *Internal Affairs*, won the BBC West of England Playwriting Competition in 1986.

Sylvia Kantaris was born in 1936 in the Derbyshire Peak District. She studied French at Bristol University, taught in Bristol and London, and then spent ten years in Australia, where she taught French at Queensland University, had two children, and wrote her MA and PhD theses on French surrealism.

In 1974 she settled in Cornwall, at Helston, and from 1976 to 1984 tutored 20th Century Poetry for the Open University. In 1986 she was appointed Cornwall's first Writer in the Community.

*

'Gross has developed a very fine narrative manner, a way of telling a story – in no matter how short a space – so that the apparently casual scatter of details and indirections of the telling finally impact with great power' – JOHN LUCAS, *New Statesman*

'Gross has a wonderful mimetic gift... In his best poems this animistic verve is allied to a sympathetic sad vision' – PETER FORBES, *The Listener*

'Kantaris is set to become one of the country's leading women poets. Her work is powerful, sensual, passionate and controlled. She avoids paltry sentimentality, and is viciously ironic when it suits her subject matter... a poet of considerable skill' – *British Book News*

'In the mainstream of her inspiration, this acute and painterly writer is unerring...Muse! send some sprigs of laurel in the direction of Helston, Cornwall' – JOHN KERRIGAN *Sunday Times*

Also by these authors

PHILIP GROSS

Familiars (Peterloo Poets, 1983)
The Ice Factory (Faber, 1984)
Cat's Whisker (Faber, 1987)
Manifold Manor (Faber, forthcoming 1989)

SYLVIA KANTARIS

Time & Motion (Prism/Poetry Society of Australia, 1975;
   repr. Menhir Press, 1986)
The Tenth Muse (Peterloo Poets, 1983; repr. Menhir, 1986)
News from the Front, with D.M. Thomas (Arc, 1983)
The Sea at the Door (Secker & Warburg, 1985)
Dirty Washing: new and selected poems (forthcoming, Bloodaxe Books,
   1989)

THE AIR MINES
of
Mistila

by
SYLVIA KANTARIS
&
PHILIP GROSS

with illustrations by
KIM LEWIS

BLOODAXE BOOKS

ISBN: 1 85224 055 5

First published 1988 by
Bloodaxe Books Ltd,
P.O. Box 1SN,
Newcastle upon Tyne NE99 1SN.

Bloodaxe Books Ltd acknowledges
the financial assistance of Northern Arts.

Typesetting by Bryan Williamson, Manchester.

Printed in Great Britain by
Bell & Bain Limited, Glasgow, Scotland.

To Geoffrey Kantaris

...for the pebble that started the landslide...

The air mines in the mountains of Mistila
Where darkness creeps into birth
Rocked by dreams of stones lapping
And dripping water like wax
Hardens into rock dripping lapping
Time measured

Where the air pulsates with the stillness of blue
Each eye lid clamped shut
Drinks the wax like meaning
Mining for air in the still vibrating blue.

[GK]

Acknowledgements

Acknowledgements are due to the editors of the following magazines in which some of these poems first appeared: *Artswest, Poetry Review, Prospice* and *Stand*.

'The Murmurings' and 'Hide-and-Seek' were inspired by hearing an account of Juan Rulfo's novel *Pedro Páramo* before their author had access to the book itself. In retrospect, the echoes appear to have been both intentional and inevitable. But for Juan Rulfo, *The Air Mines of Mistila* might never have existed, anywhere.

Contents

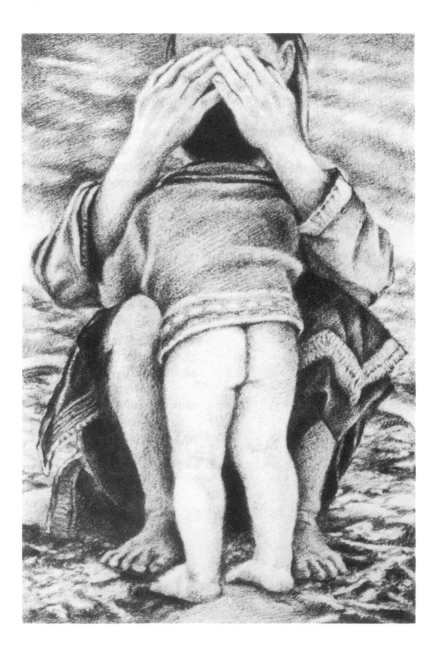

CHAPTER I

In which we stray from the marked route and a small girl's stories begin to tell themselves.

To the Air Mines of Mistila

'What tour could be complete
without a glimpse of them? Mistila's mountain air
has been mined immemorially. *The miners, it is known,*
can breathe no other. In our thriving cities of the plain
they die. It was to protect this folk our President-
            For-Life set up the Reservation.

What heart of stone would not stir
to see the lone air-miner in the dawn, setting foot
to the sheer rock wall, not to return for weeks, or ever?
Or to catch, as you depart, the glimmer of their scattered
camp fires or, faint on the wind, their old laments
            that are untranslatable and without end.

They may approach, or speak.
Take care. Their language sounds like ours
yet has different meanings. They may woo your cameras
for small gifts. It is not advisable to leave your car.
This brochure is approved by the Military Council.
            Keep to the marked route. Enjoy your stay.'

The page twitched into flame,
no warmth. Stone-dark. Chill prickling of stars.
And absences of stars, that were mountains, trees, or...
One spoke: 'You are lost.' 'Help me. Where is my car?'
'They have towed it away already. That is over. Come.'
There was a goat-hair blanket, human smells. 'Where
            are you taking me?' 'Nowhere. You are here.'

That night their breath warmed me.
The next, I ranted. They brought green bitter tea.
The next, I tried silence. Someone burred a jew's harp
out into the dark. The next, I could not sleep. 'Xencha!'
a grin beneath bush-baby eyes piped, 'Me!' She told me
      stories. I could have been the child.

How a man struck a vein of air so pure
he forgot himself and turned sculptor. With his treasure
in a goatskin bag, he left for the plain. In a roadside bar
the show: it hung for a moment, an intricate nothing in the fug,
then dissolved from the edges. They stoned him. 'Xencha,
      is this true?' 'True? Yes! For me.'

How an old man cuts deep, deeper shafts
in higher mountains, which is why he grows weary
in the body, climbing back. How they come on nubs of thunder,
this strata of human cries, the wingprints of extinct condors
fossilised in air. ('Yes,' frowns Xencha, 'you are learning
      but not perfect. Say not *they* but **we**.')

The Murmurings

Was it the murmurings that told the way to go
astray on the plateau where no one knows exactly
what is mined? (Deep down in a shaft a father's skull,
unseen but touched and cradled in the dark...)

The father lowers her deeper, deeper into pitch black –
'Search, Susan! Search! There must be more, the evidence!'
She hands up ribs, a shoulder-blade, a pelvis,
and finally the toes, joint after joint.

'There must be more than bones! Search! Search!'
(Xencha tells such tales.) It seems the dying mother said,
'Up there is where you'll find my home, the place
I loved and longed for where dreams made me thin and sere.

There are my people, high above the plain (its comforts,
its mere wheels of trees and leaves); up *there* we stored
our currency of memories.' Xencha, are you mad?
You make up so much that I can't believe or not.

She sighs, 'We all must start again.' So I must listen
to the voices of the children? 'You interrupt too much!
Stay still and hear the same voice of the mother.'
Do I hear or dream her ancient infant words?

'You will sense that up here one would wish to live forever,'
she recites. 'Dawn, morning, midday and the night,
always the same except for this one difference – the air
which changes colour with the changes of the light.

There is a draught of murmurings, as if...' She stopped.
So how can I translate what no one really said?
I agree that there were voices, whisperings – but clear?
Distilled from air? Is this the truth? (Xencha is asleep.)

The Old Man's Story

'Tell me, Grandfather, what is this lament you sing
into the darkness, night after night? Is it
for the long toil of your people? For the dwindling
of the ancient ways?' 'Your words are goatshit,

young man! Numerous but small. Oh, I could have been
a something in the world. A worshipful. A mayor.
A station master. I might afford a Model T, be seen
in a cummerbund. I could have been fat, down there.

Instead...Poor Max and me, town kids. Oh, we wished
to impress. Pure air was all the rage, those days.
We went too far, too high. We stumbled in the mist
on a miner's track. It led us suddenly no place,

a nick in the cliff. Then the cloud grew bright
and shredded, and was bright surf breaking slow
on shores of bare crags in the terrible light,
so few, so far...' 'You stayed?' 'God's blisters, no!

We scuttled home. But what had happened, what befell
our eyes. Façades and columns rustled like paper
in the breeze. Tramcars were wind-up toys, and people
nothing but suits buttoned on a curdling of shapes.

I saw a young cadet, his uniform bulging, pregnant
with a million-strong parade, flags, fists; a housewife
shopping with a cleaver in her smile; our President
orating with a baby's red-raw face that cried and cried.

I ran to Max's, but too late. I heard the shot. I saw
a raggedy smoke of starlings furling from the window
of his room, swirling and thinning out towards
the hills in a crackling sigh. I knew I had to go

where nothing pretends to be real. Where could I be
but here, the clear mists, the deceptive distances? Ah,
but my scarlet cummerbund! My fobwatch, and my Model T!
I could have been notable, and fumed on a fat cigar.'

CHAPTER II

In which the question of boundaries is aired, not for the last time, and a lady gets wind of something.

The Regulations Concerning Mist

'Mist,' say the Standing Orders (Regulations Concerning Forms of Precipitation Section 12 Para *ix*), 'should at all times be distinguished from Low Cloud. See Para *viii*.' Painstakingly

someone has pencilled: *Mist comes up. Cloud down. Sod it.* 'Less than ten yards visibility, without notification from HQ: treat as suspect, pending clarification. If in doubt, shoot...'

The sentry stiffens his moustaches. Stronger men than him have cracked up here. You can have too much Mist and Boulders (which should be distinguished from Rocks). There are snipers

everywhere, if you think. There are girls with long brown hair make sheep's-eyes at you in the dusk, then bleat and turn away the moment you get horny. And the natives sit, day after day,

watching the checkpoint, wrapped in long grey blankets, still as standing stones. You almost cease to notice them, then suddenly there's one less. And they won't perform.

They make tourists uneasy. Bad for business. But the ones you don't see are worse. They walk straight through. The wire cuts them to shreds. They reassemble slowly, like a rumour,

in the village square, through many tongues. Or in dives at dusk, by kerosene lamplight, drinkers of cloudberry wine sing them back, verse by verse, voices creeping up in time

with the moon and the mist. Or is it Low Cloud? The conscript (who should at all times be distinguished from a volunteer) shivers in his greatcoat, pulls his balaclava down. He can hear

them now, far away, and Standing Orders do not cover this.

Air Rationing

In view of the world shortage of air
occasioned by enemy interference with the atmosphere,
severe restrictions on its use will be imposed.
Starting from midnight tonight
all air will become the property of the government
and will be issued only on the production of ration books
which may be purchased from your local Air Board office.
Each person will be permitted one unit per week.
Unlicensed trading will incur severe penalties.
Any person or persons discovered using air
for other than essential purposes
will be liable to instant confiscation of ration books.

'What shall we do about it, Lischka?
It's our livelihood. What have we got
but air?' She's miles away, absorbed
in a tattered *Beano*. 'It appears,'
she says, 'they need their air to pump up
small balloons with *Zonk! Ouch! Yoicks!*
and rows of little stars. Big men need big
balloons. We'll go directly to the top –
inflated words. Now let's get down to work.'

We couldn't think, but she came up with
Free World, The People, Democracy, the Truth,
Almighty God, strategical, defence, my wife,
and sent them to our President-For-Life
in spite of Ezreq who stormed off in protest
and hammered an enormous slab of air to pulp.

Lischka says each bubble we puffed up
has been used since (without acknowledgement).
Ezreq says our gifts are dangerous. We must
step up our underground activities.
Lischka's pocketing pure air because
it sells like needles in the market place.

The Myth of Lischka

Lischka stepped down through the pass without a permit.
We say we made her up. It was the way she spun air
into curios (needles' eyes so fine they seemed to melt
on sight, and broderies more delicate than mist)
that caught our breath. She got a good price sometimes
down there in the market place (depending on the light).
'Say please Sir, thank you Sir, and spread your legs.'
We heard the thunder of the camera flash.
Sometimes she used to bring back beans and wax,
and once there was a nothing in a plastic bag
that wriggled for a while, then stopped.
Lischka learnt their language and commuted,
barefoot. Beware of rumours that she still exists.

Here in the Reservation we survive, at least.
We mine and are provided for. The air is rare.
Lischka brought us words that were difficult to hear,
though Lomu shapes a rifle butt, as if...
(He doesn't really mean it. Only lies are truth.)
We women whisper, spinning by the bluelight.
Old Jasta wastes breath, keening in the night.
All the people up here in Mistila are made up,
like Lischka. Lischka is a myth, we tell
the travellers we find, lost, following her footsteps.
We frisk them for their dictionaries of common usage,
try to learn their phrase books off by heart.
I can recite, 'Stop thief!' and 'Officer, this scoundrel
has attempted at my inlaid pigskin purse.'

The Chief of Police's Tale

There she sat, hawking her nothings in *my* market square
among the goat-butchers, grog-shops, lentil-dumpling-
vendors (crooks to a man but at least they sell *something*,
if only a hangover). Why had nobody reported her?

'Why?' I shouted. They shuffled and muttered. She sat,
empty-handed, bare legs in the dust. Of course! No-
where but in this gopher hole would men stoop so low,
to touch one of *them*. 'Take her away,' I spat.

'Where, Sir? The jail has fallen down.' I had her shut
in the one safe house. My own. There she would see my gun,
my brass medal (from the old régime), see I was *someone*
not to be snubbed with the dumb blue stare. 'Slut!'

I cried, 'What do you charge them for your...services?'
She emptied her bag: six beans, a nail, some amber wax,
a penny whistle...'Each pays with what they have.
So will you.' 'Hussy! Don't forget whose house this is!

When my wife comes from the city she will smell the smell.
Go wash. Make yourself decent.' I never meant...But there
she stood, in night-sky black, seed-pearls for stars:
my mother's mourning dress. I slapped her and she fell

across the bed. 'Bitch!' As I straddled her, curiously
numb, I was high, breathless, near vertigo, hacking away
at something cold but insubstantial. It gave. As I came,
I lost my grip. I fell. I would fall for ever. 'Help me'

stretched from my lips. I clutched about to find her
gone. Only the black dress, stained, torn, rumpled.
And a tapping at the locked door: 'Sir? Is there struggle?
Please, what are my orders? What has become, Chief Sir?'

The Tale of the Wife of the Chief of Police

Normally the house smells of *Aerosol*
but last night I was met by the stench of absence.
He'd cleared up the traces but I sensed the guilt.
'You've had *her* here again, you pig!' I screamed.

Of course *he* said I was a stupid sow, a bitch
who dreamed up evidence that never did exist,
scratching his neck under the collar till it bled
a red stain on his shirt. I crossed myself

and challenged him to prove his innocence,
but it was as I thought. He couldn't do it.
'I'm tired, I've got a headache,' he complained.
I knew who'd drained him of his essences.

That tramp, that trollop from the mountain
in her see-through flimsy nothings had seduced him
for the price of a missing pack of seeds
with her airy-fairy words that make no sense.

I've heard whispers though and once, late at night,
there was a rustle in the alleyway. I couldn't
grasp the meaning but I caught the drift
and tried to write it, but it melted in the process.

I know nothing, never caught a glimpse.
What would become of us if we were all bewitched?
Who would man the jails? My husband's medal
for his services to law and order is already tarnished.

Alys and the Oral Tradition

My love came from the mountains
He has done me right and wrong
I know not him nor yet my child
And my time will not be long.

Dusk. The village draws into itself, and apart:
here, a lit window; there, a door opens and shuts;
a child is shushed; dogs yap from yard to yard,
and someone is singing. Alys stands. She would be
a shadow if she could, the long black shawl
across her face. If Max passed now, he would see
nobody, another peasant. But hush, that song...

So dark he stood at the courtyard gate
The wind wiped away his song
A drink, he begged, my throat is dry
I shall not hold you long.

His hair was like some storm cloud
His hands both kind and strong
He bent his lips to my earthen bowl
And drank there deep and long.

Maxwell had knelt once: 'Be my First Lady. A Chief
of Police is a somebody. His wife is a somebody else.'
The jeep could run her into town. Do not lose your chic,
he said. And later, don't spend your time with nobodies.
Except on official occasions. Don't be seen without a hat.
He was out at pistol practice. She could hear the peevish
peck of his gun up the hillside. And the song...

There's nowhere in the world, he said
Our baby will belong
But I'll return the day he is born
And take my child along.

Behind that wall would be a garden, and a slim girl singing her heart away straight to the sky. The Alys-shadow peeped. There, by an iron mangle was a terrible gross woman lading washing. As she slapped a shirt and trousers off the stone, a brief male outline dried away. The pistol-swats had stopped. Run. As she turned the hag threw back her head and a pure voice sang...

Now the night comes from the mountains
And I know not right nor wrong
Where is my love? Where is my child?
My time will not be long.

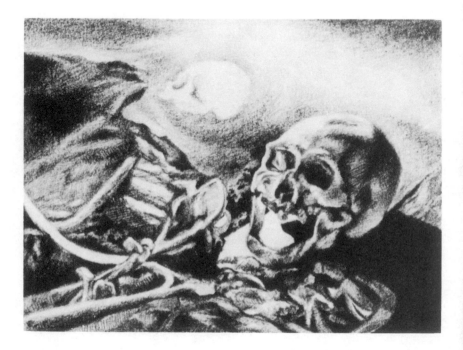

CHAPTER III

In which a young man ventures into the world, and an old one out of it.

Lomu and the Spirits

Lomu go
fetch water, go
watch goat, now
pot boil over,
Ma bawl, Pa
dumb, he blunt
his fingerbones
break stones
for what?
shit, no!

Lomu go
all right
where autos purr
pick spot to watch
like mountain fox
in picnic place
Coke hotdog crisp
what this?
tin-glittery
a chitter-box

Lomu love the thing
has spirits in
all night
they party-hop they sing
speak tongues to him
until
    they croak
quick! wave truck down
'spirits sick' 'Jump in'
driver wiseman grin
drop him in town

                              Lomu stop
                              glass bottle shop
                              'spirits quick!'
                              gets oily water
                              Lomu dry like brick
                              he drink
                              now man come
                              open palm
                              'but spirits sick!'
                              open palm come fist

box bust, street
catch him, spin
him round, he sing
he speak in tongues
spirits free and fine
till
        boots thump 'Scum!'
run, headlights, rain
beat down 'Go home'
(spirits sick in pain)
'Thief! Mountain bum!'

A Ritual

Jasta is gone.
Tomorrow we will feed
his body to the air.
We are weaving his cradle.

Tonight there is haste.
He went without a word
watching for his dole
of cactus porridge, the ladle

dripping. He forgot
so many little things
he will be sure to miss
when he arrives. So Xencha

little one must run
being young and supple-
soft to squirm through openings
too small for sense.

We sway her in a circle.
We rock her from arm to arm.
This is the Hive of Ghosts;
we swathe her in a nasal hum

till her big eyes close. 'Now,
little meltwater minnow,
run!' Her mother whispers.
'Overtake the old one

on the steep track.
Remind him of our names.
Say we sigh good air for him.
Say his goats go well. And say

here are his tools, the noun
whetstone, the verb *to sprag*.
Also *dirigible* and *flim-flam*:
he will want to play.

Give him his treasure.
Then – oh watch for the way
and the footing – hurry back.'
Unsurely, Xencha stands,

as if for blind-man's buff.
She threads a maze between
no obstacles to where he lies.
She folds into his hands

his nickel-plated key-ring
with the ritual words
worn smooth by fingering:
FORD MOTORS.

With it, he used to say,
if he had not mislaid the key,
he would open all our doors.
If we had doors.

Post Mortem

The question's simple: what did Xencha see?
Lomu wants to understand. His head
hurts with it. Old Jasta's gone,
they tell him. 'How? And where?'

But Xencha's in a playful mood:
'Ask no questions, you'll get no lies.'
'But why?' he asks, 'Why do people die?'
'Y's a stupid letter and Z's no better,'

she sings, and twirls her skirt and giggles,
'Let's play In-And-Out-The-Dusky-Bluebells.'
Lomu wants to argue but can't focus:
'*Dusty* would be better than *dusky*,' he groans.

A final effort: 'Xencha, please explain.'
She spells it out: Oh, *flim-flam* then!
Sprag off! Go play with a *dirigible!*' He frowns,
'You know I never did like Sticks-and-Stones.'

Hide-and-Seek

He wriggled through a little gap
between old planks and balanced for a minute,
then down he went, dangling like a puppet.
'Lower! Lower! Search!' the old man called,
funnelling his voice. Lomu heard it.
The light beam danced, then focussed.
'It's a dead man's skull!' he cried.

The jawbone broke off in his hand like sugar-icing
from a birthday cake. He held the round bowl
of the cranium as if to drink his fill of dust.
It crumbled. There was nothing else –
just echoes in the shaft of his own throat.

After many days and nights of ice
he met the stone stare of the old man's face,
and laughed, 'I knew where you were hiding
all along, before you even hid!'

CHAPTER IV

In which the difficulty of talking to people is equalled only by the difficulty of not doing so.

Ul'ma and the Other One

Xencha touches his shoulder. She kneels with a gourd of gruel.
'Watch,' Ul'ma points, 'Now she feeds him. She is more like
mother to him than child. And after, they will sit. And she –
you know her prattling – she won't breathe...' 'He talks to her?

I thought...' 'It is as you thought. He has lost his words.'
She lays her faggot of thorn-twigs down. 'Even his name.
It was up on the old High Level. We warned him: the weight
of years is too much, the rock's wormy with worked-out shafts.

He would go. And then it came, hardly a sound, more a crumbling in
of air: a thunder-slip! And worse, the settling of the hush
that buried it. Four days we scratched for a sign of him.
We turned for home; that's when he stepped out of nowhere

as if through a door, and stared at us. Now the most he does
is smile – but not foolishly, no – as if hearing all we say
translated to a foreign language, and approving of the style.
No name will stick to him now. We fashion him another

and repeat it to him, slowly, and by evening every one
of us has forgotten it. He has become, simply, The Other One.
Work? Him? He's a student of stone. I fetch and stoop,
I scrub and grind, and sometimes I look up and there,

at his special stone, he sits and stares. I round on him,
"What sort of husband are you? What use?" and...yes,
our Xencha...*she* came from a moment like this – that gaze
opens out for me, like a deep cool cave. I step in...'

Lomu's Peace-Effort

Lomu struck an impure vein of air
so stained with fear, he hammered it for months
and finally emerged with his arsenal.
'It's time to cut the cackle,' he asserted,
then took a year deliberating.
Which of his weapons would be most effective?
In the end, he judged by sound. 'The cloudmongers
will understand once they hear *this*,' he said.
We had to let him go. He disappeared
down through the mist with an empty backpack.

Three clouds later he returned, downcast.
Nobody had understood his sounds, he said.
No one had clapped except a deaf old woman
who had written seven books on primroses
and hoped Lomu could help her get them published.
The Chief of Police had moved him on.
'Get back up there to the Reservation
where your kind belong, else I'll charge you
with acting under false pretences.'

                              'Waste of breath!'
says Ezreq, 'Nothing happened. What did you expect?'

The Other One's Soliloquy

              stone   still
        mind a stone   that stone on that stone
balancing   so fulcral   cantilevered   canting leaving NO
       no canting   still it   stone

                    good
       safer   mind a stone   dumb   peace-
ful   full of pieces NO   stone full of stone   stone
seamed with ore   stone full of seeming   full of either/or
       eider down   white feathers   drifting down
              NO   still it   stone

                    Xencha   there
       shares stone   my little   mine
full of ore   says nothing   waiting   weighting down
NO   wait   maybe one word NO   word breeds word go wild I
       know   going under going   thunder   NO
              safer   still as stone

                    one word   one   *dear?*
       dare? NO   let one loose and NO one is safe
you think it's only *goat* or *bowl*   then it's *dear*   soon enough
it'll be   *rampant fulgent zygote*   too late then   the monsters
grazzle morbulent bruntiminy   who'll put them back who'll lock
       them in   like rock like stone like rocking NO
              undermined   hush   lock it   stone

                    Xencha
              leaving   leaving no
       word said   wait   no   be a stone
still   stone still   still   but   still

Ezreq

'...is difficult,' they said, 'We trade our breath
here easily, for little ends, to give, take, touch. Ezreq
eats apart and sets out before dawn. Ezreq is strong and scarred
and has been where tracks run out, beyond...Yet, who knows?
If you must question, she may talk to you.'

She glanced up, giving nothing with her face,
then back to what her fingers twined and finicked, finer,
quicker. An hour or more, I watched it hummed and muttered
into shape. Then her cracked navvy's palm thrust it up to me,
too small to make out. She nodded, 'Now.'

'The work,' I said, 'How is it done? And why?
I have to understand.'
                            'Your words defeat you, friend! Have,
and you will never understand. Understand, and you have not.'
'The others tell me what they can.'
                                        '*Can* is too much. Earth
is too small for it. Say what you must.'

How could I? 'Forgive me. I will go.'
                                        'Wait.
Once, out beyond, I found an aviator in his wrecked machine
among the rocks. Its wings were hollow stalks and dry seed-pods
of whisper-grass. His face in its mask was yours. Do you fly?'
'No. Never.'
                'Then perhaps you will.'

'Beyond?'
            'Where is *beyond*, once you are there?
But you will ask. That cave of grime and ice where the glacier
unlocks, drip by drip...That would cure you of your questions.'
'What did you see?'
                        'A child in party frills, her face blackened
but preserved. You have guessed? It was mine.

But the work? Forced labour, year on year.
Then one day without warning drop your tools, let your hands
open as if to beg, or to lift a bowl (hush now, hold it still)
to the lips of a thirsty stranger. So hard, yet so easy. See,
your hands are empty. Yet they fill.'

CHAPTER V

In which a scholarly mind is brought to bear on the situation, but some questions have no answers.

Dr Crampfold's Complaint

Dear Sirs, While sensible of the trust your august institution has
    reposed in me
I have to report that my contribution to the *World Digest of Critical*
    Socio-Philology
will be delayed. My expenses here are nil, as are my findings. This –
    can one strictly call
it a "community"? – has nothing one might properly term a *custom*.
    I have explained to them that all
known cultures have such things. They express surprise, or interest
    (or are simply polite)
and say 'You are a great professor of this. Teach us. May we do a
    custom this very night?'
Their dialect appears a hybrid of the common tongue and an
    uncommon desire to confound.
'Our roots are in air,' they say, 'The leaves reach the earth and
    brush it with a speaking sound.'
The deep structure of their grammar resembles the labyrinths of
    shafts, mostly disused,
that litter these slopes. 'The wind,' they say, 'strays into them and
    cries aloud confused
like a hundred whales.' They have never seen a whale. They have
    forty words for a certain bean
they never cat. 'Forty beans make only wind,' they say, 'Please tell
    us what we mean.'

A Custom

We must have a *Custom*, Dr Crampfold says.
Otherwise we won't fit in the *World Digest*
of Socio-Philosophy. It's critical.
Dr Crampfold won't get his expenses
until we think one up. We'll have to choose.
It seems we're not allowed to mention whales.
'Why not?' asks Xencha, 'What's wrong with a whale?'
'Describe one, then' (Lomu). 'Okay,' she says.
We wait while she goes into silence.
'Fat lot of good *you* are,' says Poppinlock,
pronouncing his very first words. (We'd thought
that Poppinlock would never speak.) It turned out
he was waiting, politely, to be asked
for his opinion, but he grew incensed:
'About bloody time we had a custom!'
That was his second try at grouping words.
'Invent one for us, Poppinlock,' we begged.
He thought a bit and frowned. A little forehead
shouldn't have to be so old and crinkled,
but he came up with the goods: 'Let's suppose
we dance a Rain Dance dating from the Reindeer Age.'
We'd never heard of this, but Dr Crampfold
took off to a library to do research
and came back triumphant. 'I've found it!'
he shouted, 'You are customised at last!'
It seems we were calcated just before
the Neolithic. Poppinlock went dumb.
Xencha said, 'The air is full of customs,
some of which we haven't even thought of yet.'
All of us expressed our gratitude
to Dr Crampfold. He has put us on the map.

The Lie of the Land

Tap. Tap. Who?
What? There's a man on hands and knees
attacking the hillside with a little hammer.
      'Not today, thank you,'
      says Ul'ma, 'We like our hill
just the way it is.' 'Oh, pardon me,'
he looks up, blinking, 'I'm a collector.
      Rocks. Yours are remarkable.
      Metamorphic, of course.'
'But of course!' brags Poppinlock,
'Never the same view two days running!'
      (All these tourist brochures,
      they're affecting his style.)
'Springs gush forth from the barren rock!
Old sources fail. The fulsome, photogenic
      Isabella Guzman waterfall
      became a staircase overnight
when some workings subsided and the tarn
was swallowed whole. Goose feathers scattered
      upstream came to light
      weeks later in the taps
of the new motel. Also...' he pauses
for effect, 'white deposits, analysed as bone –
      some mouse, some bat,
      some definitely human.'
There's a shudder of nods and whispers:
'Ezreq at her work again', 'Must be something
      to do with Susan.'
      One of Xencha's stories
tells of the man who stayed below
in the exhausted seams, lifelong librarian
      of the endless galleries,
      cross-referencing ghosts.
Blind and pale, he picks his way by touch
or echo...But the collector's bag is full.
      At the Customs Post
      it is emptied on the floor
and impounded. 'Everything you've seen
or heard – forget it!' And the guilty specimens,

heavy with glints of ore,
are spirited away. Where
does the trail lead? Up, from desk to desk,
till a President-For-Life in his Polaroid shades
can contemplate the glare?
Or down? Are they found
by a trash-picker on the smouldering
city dump? Sold for a song? Or leaked, translated,
smuggled underground?

The One That Got Away

Poppinlock sits fishing in a disused shaft.
He's caught nothing in his net but spinks
for weeks. What's he after? He says, 'Sticklebacks.'
We shrug but say politely that we like the sound.
'I expect he'll catch a whale,' says Xencha.
(There are a lot of whales now in Mistila
since Xencha introduced them. Every time
the clouds open, we say it's raining whales.
It is our "custom". Dr Crampfold's pleased
and is writing a thesis on our whale cult.)
But Lischka's adamant and says that whales
are not abstract enough for Poppinlock
and anyway he favours polysyllables –
'Remember how he loved Jasta's *dirigibles*.'
We all did, but they're Jasta's and he's gone
and taken his dirigibles with him,
so we can't have them. It would be indecent.
'Derivative,' says Ul'ma, and nods.
Meanwhile Poppinlock's just sitting, pondering.
His mother's scared in case he goes too deep
and gets lost in the labyrinth.
Sigh after sigh escapes us in advance.
(Elegies are everybody's favourites.)
We miss him deeply – all his silences,
his footsteps and the gaps between his fingers,
the little space between us and his back,
and all the words he might have caught but for

36

the one word on the tip of his breath
that slips like Jasta's shadow through the net.
'Is this a custom?' Dr Crampfold asks,
'How does it relate to the whale cult?'
'We're wailing red herrings,' Xencha answers
helpfully, 'Or maybe crocodiles?'
Poppinlock's mother fancies crocodiles
but says that pterodactyls would be
more acceptable in elegies.

A Crossing

'Where are you taking me?' I said, 'To find my car? Home?
    Through the wire?'
                        'Some can slip through,'
my strange guide said, 'but you...? You lack the art
    of truthfully seeming. Perhaps for you
the way is underground. Careful! Here it narrows. We must crawl.'

I tracked his slight warmth in the cold and dark. A chink
    of white dazzle broke in high
through a fissure. Puddles and grit: we went by touch.
    'Better not to see,' he said. Sometimes
the air pressed near, sometimes rang with vaults or drops.

Once I felt him stiffen: 'Hush,' he said, 'We come
    to the Babel Chamber. Any single word
will be echoed in every known language and more unknown.
    Be warned. What men have heard
here takes away their taste for meaning. Then they starve.'

Hours on, a shock of light...I hauled out on black scree
    but my guide lagged behind.
I turned and faced him then. 'Did the Surface Folk
    not tell you?' he said, 'I am blind.'
Low cloud shuffled sedge and boulders. 'What do you see?'

A bird marked its track overhead with a dull *cack-coing*
    like a rusty bedspring. Then again
some boulders flounced and shuddered off: wild horses,
    rope-maned, lips bared, blown away
like smoke. At last, 'A house!' – a thickening of mist

into a drystone stump, just enough to frame one thin
    arched window. Cloud-frost on our hair,
we shivered in a hearth-pit. Rusted to the one wall
    was a branding iron, a fetter. 'Where
are you leading me?' I asked again. He shook his head.

I stared till the dimness blotched and tattered back
    onto a harder grey: a ploughed field
to the horizon, scrawled by many tractors. In a ditch
    I saw one clear: a tank, keeled
turret down as if to drink, charred to the same grey.

'You see?' he said, 'You wish to cut your way home
    short?' 'But is all this...true?'
'All men's short cuts end much like this. Besides,
    we had no guide but you.
And now,' he tightened on my sleeve, 'Which way is home?'

CHAPTER VI

In which a lady receives something for nothing, or does she?

Alys and the Oral Tradition II

It must be the altitude. No zing, no zip.
Maxwell has to face facts. The marching band
is a failure. They would rather just sit
huffing those throaty pipes. Too much wind
from the mountains. And those majorettes!
'Alys?' She's in the dark, her back to him,
at the open window; her lips trace a song.

She turns slowly with a brightness in her eye
that disturbs him. 'Max,' she breathes, 'If I gave
you a bowl of water, would you drink?' 'Am I
a dog? I have a six-pack in the fridge. You know
the water's not safe. What's got into you?'
'Max, try to understand. Several months ago
something happened. I think it was the song.

There's no one else, I swear. And you know we
haven't, you know...' His hand is on his holster.
'And since then I haven't...Well, it's been
four months. Max, you must believe.' The white
feather hat that she never would wear stirs
to a cool night breeze, as if it might just fly.
She cradles her belly. 'A miracle. It was the song!'

Max and the Muse

Bare legs in the dust again,
bare brown legs in the dust –
my gypsy thief, my tinker from the mountain,
how can I speak my love, my heart, my mistress?

Asking for it are you, slag?
What's in your bag? Unzip!
And do something about your hair.
My wife is pregnant.

Get a move on, bitch! Quick smart!
And keep your trap shut.
My wife wears hats.
Spill the lot out. Show me all your trash.

(Same as always – three beans,
two nails and a bit of amber wax.
What the hell am I supposed to do with *that*?)
I said MY WIFE IS PREGNANT! Are you deaf?

Slattern, strumpet, tart!
Why can't you just look decent?
Your skirt rucked up, your hair a mess of ragwort…
I've warned you once. My wife wears hats.

Bare legs in the dust again,
bare brown legs in the dust –
my gypsy thief, my tinker from the mountain,
how can I speak my love, my heart, my Alys?

Sprag! Crank! Get out!
Shift back up there, tramp! Rag-bag!
My wife is pregnant
and my wife wears hats.

Xencha's Pets

The smiling tiger-shrew would dance its prey
to a trance, then chop! It brought her lacy butterflies
alive in its teeth. It tickled her ear on slaughter day
when the billy-kids were culled. It liked the eyes.

The velvety hermit bat swayed from the rafters
above her bed. Its plug-ugly mug giggled upside down.
The adults couldn't hear. 'I saw your great-grandfather's
bones today. Looks well, considering.' News from underground.

The snow-goose called her, crying south, each year
for a day, to the same grey tarn. There she would stand.
It preened and shook. She would read her people's future
in feathers, how they floated, where they came to land.

The shrew died tangling with its own reflection
in a Cadillac's chrome. The bat pursued its echo – *I*,
I – through the worked-out mine. The goose did not come.
The Chief of Police gave his wife a hat which made her cry

unlike Xencha. She hugs her knees. Her tongue
tastes words with a sour metallic thrill like nothing
she has known: 'I have many pets now. Come, little one.'
Snug in her palm, a stone winks, darkly, glittering.

CHAPTER VII

In which the world is too much with us, but a star is born.

Protect and Survive

Lischka came back this time with a faded leaflet
and a word we couldn't grasp. It was "holocaust".
P. thought it sounded like a swarm of locusts
but we'd never seen a locust and in any case
Lischka was in earnest: 'Shut up for once!
What we need are tins and tins of whitewash
to paint the windows at the moment of the flash.'
Unfortunately, though, we have no windows
and Poppinlock insisted on playing the goat:
'Could we paint ourselves instead? That is,
if we could find ourselves? If we had whitewash?'
Lischka withered him with a single glance:
'I was about to say that we need windows first,
before I was so rudely interrupted. Once
we have the windows we are safe – if we have whitewash;
also *doors*. We need doors to rip out,
otherwise we can't make an inner retreat.'
We looked up *door* and *inner* and *retreat*
and found a lot of fruitful synonyms, but
Lischka kept on being serious. It was life or death.
Why, though, since we're harmless and quite useless?
Nobody would ever want to cancel us out,
apart from which we even have a rent book.
Lischka said our rent book made no difference
and listed all the items that we needed:
cans of beans, a radio, and water for three weeks
plus a bucket and a lot of disinfectant.
We took stock: 3 beans, 2 goats and a scrap of wax.
It wouldn't do; we had to have lace curtains
to tear down from the windows we don't have
and quickly paint the latter with whitewash,
and then unhinge the doors we don't possess,

in about the time it takes a goat to cough.
'Okay,' says Poppinlock, 'it's obvious – if we have
no curtains, windows, doors or whitewash, none of us
will ever get to see a holocaust, so what's the point?'

A Communication: First Draught

Dear Mr Minister, your honour,
Dr Crampfold say you no yet understand our lingo
but we good kids from Mistila, yes sir.
Dr Crampfold ~~learn us~~ teach us
read write and add up to something else.
We got rent book now and customs,
also double-glazing but no windows
Sir is why I ask you windows please.
We simple folk, no kidding. Man wants job
most desperate fix windows under double-glazing
so we shift fog, keep air outside
of our insides, learn to see straight.
And my brother he say we need door as well,
then we be respectable as hell,
keep bad spirits downstairs locked up.
(My brother has bad spirits once
but now he see not bad.)
We in mortal fear of draughts, Sir,
since the Whitewash. We no whitewash yet
but we pay rentbook beans. No dice?

Zamon and the Big Time

Yes, Ezreq had a child – who knows how? Quick little spink
he was. Set him to watch the goats, he'd weave their bleats
in lovers' knots hung from their tails so they ran in circles.
It was all a joke to Zamon. Yes, *the* Zamon. But that came later.

Myself, I blame the Cigarillo Man. His Buick came grinning
to the verge where Zamon squatted playing Tower of Hanoi
with a little pyramid of echoes. 'Say, can you do that again?
You can? Hop in, kid. I can make you big big big…'

The critics popped their corks. 'Such insubstantiality!
The art form we've been waiting for. To call it minimal
would be too gross. It refers purely to nothing.' Students
purchased Zamon T-shirts and went naked to the waist.

One night a stage hand blundered. The curtain rose; the stage
was empty. The crowds cheered as one man. 'His masterpiece!
Such ontological finesse!' Backstage, he overheard. He ran.
His last creation meeped as it was eaten by the extractor fan.

*

'Say, aren't you Zamon?' 'No, I just look like him.' 'Like?
Look? No one says *like* any more. We're all post-Zamonists now,
kid. Where have you been?' 'Please, which road to Mistila?'
The barman laughed, 'Mistila? No such place. Zamon invented it.

You aren't into Zamon? You've got to hear his new LP –
Zamon Live. Drink this while I crank the phonograph…'
The black disc's silence sizzled on like rain. A crack
went spink! spink! The barman's eyes went so faraway

he didn't see the boy slumped weeping, didn't even hear
the door crash in. Two bulging heavies flanked
the Cigarillo Man, who champed: 'It's all fixed. Yes, kid,
the international tour. The world is ready for you now.'

A Problem of Ownership

'Who owns Mistila?' is the question in the air.
Lischka brought new words on faded paper
and we read between the dots. First we belonged
to this tribe, and then that; were claimed,
acclaimed and reclaimed, told to speak up,
keep quiet, shut up. One of them protests:
'Mistila was a long gift from our ancestors.'
The other says, 'So what? We have invested
in the mines which are strategic, and minorities
must therefore be protected.' Even the wind
is divided. Lomu shapes a hand-grenade and means it.
'There will be ash here, also,' Xencha forecasts.

Jasta used to say that if we shaped gods,
gods would eat us up. But he was wracked
and raddled with mythologies and key-rings
and spoke goatshit. We learn new ways now,
gamble on results, and Lomu's fixed
a big blow-football match
to keep our fighting spirits up to scratch.

CHAPTER VIII

In which we learn to tell lore from law, and words from deeds.

Who Owns Mistila?

1 *Deed*

'In the beginning was [   ],
so much, all the [   ] there could be,
for all the time there was. Then suddenly
    it blinked.

That was it – the deed,
the something that set echo blurring echo
into…' 'Please,' pipes Poppinlock, 'I know.
    It was a spink.'

Xencha tweaks him: 'Go
knit your own myth.' 'But I know. I saw!'
'Saw? What d'you think this is? A court of law?'
    'As a matter of fact,'

sighs the judge, 'it is. Though where
this bears on title deeds I have yet to see.
Let him proceed.' 'Thank you, your Expectancy.
    So the [   ] cracked…'

'Wait! Will someone tell me,'
cries the Clerk, 'how to spell [   ]?' 'Don't
use words, for a start. Besides, it was a goat,
    not a spink. It coughed.'

Uproar in court. 'If you won't
believe me, try imagining NO GOATS. Well?
There you are!' 'Order. Let the witness tell
    his tale.' 'There was this soft

zzzummmm. It was a B.
The note, I mean,' the old man strops a glance
round the gallery, 'Then it began to dance.
        What else could it do?'

    The judge raps, 'Documents
are what concern us. Words.' 'Ah, words. Eventually –
I will pass over the three-tone scale, polyphony,
        the art of fugue –

    some sounds congealed, grew sticky
to things as in *flapjack, gunk.* Or hung between
things as in *wheedle, sprag, careen.*
        So on, through *goods* and *mine*

    to *status quo, inevitable, has-been.*
Then we opened our mouths to speak, and knew
we were naked: *zero-rated, low on follow-through*
        as of this time.

    (And that was only the beginning.)'

2   *Point of Order*

'These people can in no real sense be called
a *people.* I refer you to Crampfold pp.58
to 63. They wander at will, inventing festivals
as they go. They never meet together.'
                                'Except now!'

The crowd nods. 'You mean this is all
of you?' frowns the judge. 'Yes, every last one.
Except Ezreq.' 'Count them!' 'But Your Honour,'
the Clerk hems, 'Don't think I haven't tried.

They are always a different number.' 'Who
is the leader?' Shrugs and shuffles. 'Very well,
the oldest?' A quick buzz, then...'Muz'mul?
Does anyone remember Muz'mul being born?'

'I do,' a frail voice ventures. 'Facts at last!
Your name?' 'Why, Muz'mul, sir.' 'Never mind.
How many of your...people are there?' 'Where, sir?'
'Here.' 'Why, sir, *all*. Except Ezreq.'

'Your Honour,' the Clerk fumbles, 'May I draw
your attention to Crampfold appendix D: "The Game
of Numbers in Mistila". He makes reference to, er,
the Parable of the Goat Droppings.'
                                        '*Well?*'

the judge glares round very slowly.
                            'Oh, that one!
Dr Crampfold found it underneath a thornbush. How
did it go? We have a literary style called *Snow-
in-April* – much flutter, from a great height,

leaving no impression. I remember that we laughed
like...like...Like geysers!' 'I must caution you.
There are no geysers in Mistila.' 'Quite so,
Your Exactitude. Yes, we laughed like whales.'

3 *Lore*

> '*In the reign of Tuscan Hyde*
> *I crept through a crack in Mumma's side*
> *In the reign of Clashman Ward*
> *Sowed fool's gold and reaped a sword...*'

(The judge shifts, 'Is there a great deal of this?' 'The Defence intends
to establish the tribe's antiquity. Note the reference to the Reindeer
Age.')

> '*In the reign of Potson Pan*
> *Sold red rust to the stovepipe man*
> *In the reign of Sad Nick Mills*
> *Turned the innards out of our hills...*'

('Who is this pebble-brain?' says Xencha. 'An expert, dear.' 'An ex
what?' 'Someone who used to be pert.' 'Oh, I see.')

> *In the reign of Puffin Blow*
> *All Ma's children working down below*
> *In the reign of Gopher Broke*
> *Grow old quick with the coffin-choke...*'

('The text is corrupt, of course.' The archivist buffs his pince-nez.
'Then again, what can you expect of an oral tradition?')
   'In the reign of Allwork Doubt
   No one nowhere getting nowt
   In the reign of Awfull Down
   Deep in the shafts I heard a sound...'
('He's flat!' hisses Xencha, 'What a flake of schist!' 'Hush,' whispers
Ul'ma, 'This one is on our side. I think.')
   'In the reign of Mumma Rings
   These were the words I heard her sing
   NOTHING HERE BUT WIND AND REIGN
   BLOW IT ALL AWAY AND START AGAIN.'
(But Xencha is on the podium. 'No, no. You've got to *skip*. Pick up
your feet. Look! I should know. I only made it up last week.')

4   Last Word

Professor V. Torquiss, Honorary Dean
of the President Guzman Institute of Philosophy
pats his corrugated silver hair:
'The logic of the case is child's play. It is this.
How can an entity, a real thing, exist?

By being defined! A thing *sans* boundaries
is no thing (or everything, which is absurd). These
people have been asked: what are the limits
of Mistila? See, they shrug. How can one own
what one cannot limit? One man alone,

our leader, whose concretely philosophic mind
conceived of wall and wire, yes, *he* has defined
Mistila. It is his. I rest my case.' His chess-
fiend's smile extends. And locks rigid. The door
bangs open. 'Esmeralda!' 'Valentine! But call

me Ezreq.' 'Order in court! Professor Torquiss,'
the judge clutches at his gavel, 'Do you *know* this...
person?' Ezreq hooshes him aside: 'Case? Nothing
is the case. Only fables. Here is one. It starts
in '68. The students seize the Faculty of Arts.

Free love (a young don lectures them on lechery)
breaks the banks. Fuck, and conceive of history!
Meanwhile who plucks the cobblestones? Who raids
Sculpture for the chisels? Who breaks in
to Music to string crossbows out of violins?

To whom, as the riot police smoke out the campus
(wreaths of tear gas rising bridal, luminous),
does this intellectual sigh: *My brute antithesis!*
Transcend our contradictions! Take me! as the wall
caves in? Armoured bulldozers grin in from the hall.

They take him in his underpants. They don't yet know
the army changed sides overnight. He is a hero
of the Revolution. He is Honorary Dean. And she?
She bore the child, then she exchanged hot air
for cool mist. Where does Mistila start, where

end?' But the judge is blushing. 'Case dismissed!'

The Reindeer Age

It snowed reindeer for centuries, the air
was thick with reindeer, we grew reindeer
upon reindeer, layer on layer and year on year,
and yet the sky still lowered.

We were blanketed in reindeer, climbed
the reindeer hills, spake Reindeer,
dressed in reindeer, bartered reindeer
for reindeer, milled the bones with bones.

On reindeer beds we dreamed in Reindeer, drank
the blood and ate the flesh and read the Reindeer Scriptures,
heads bowed in the Temple of the Antlers.
'In the beginning was the Stag,' we chanted.

The reindeer grazed on reindeer and on us,
as we on them and on each other. We were all the same,
made in the image of the Oneness of the Stag.
And when He sent His Fawn we ate Him also.

It was Paradise until the Fall.
One day there was a sudden hail of stones
(which introduced the Neolithic Age).
Thereafter we ate stone and worshipped Stone.

But some of us remembered and recorded the Scriptures
on new-fangled pebbles, taking care to scatter them
like disconnected accidents or dice.
The intercalcation took all night.

We didn't count the cost, we planted *Truth*
under the first layer of the Neolithic,
gambling with our lives to leave the indexed evidence
for future historians to collate.

Letter to *The Historical Times*, January 1930.

Sir – I am astounded to find that the only reference to the Reindeer Age in
the new (1929) *Encyclopaedia Britannica* (see under 'Pebble Writing') is both
scant and dismissive. Clearly the "historian" does not believe the markings on
the pebbles (intercalcated between the last layer of the Reindeer Age and the
first of the Neolithic Period) to have been mere accidents of weathering, though
'scattered about without relation or connection', as he says. How are we to
understand from this precisely what happened when the Neolithic Age replaced
the Reindeer Age? I abhor the suggestion that the stones may have been used
in playing games or *gambling*. – Crampfold.

The Meeting

Lomu calls a meeting to propose a meeting:
'What's the point of being here together if we're not?
We haven't even got an agenda.' Xencha fidgets.
He digs his heels in: 'We'll take minutes.'
'We *are* together, though,' (Poppinlock).
'Prove it, then! Describe me!' Lomu bridles,
'To start with, what's the colour of my hair?'
Xencha skips in quick: 'It's either reindeer,
stickleback or spink or water or...'
'You're balder than an antler or a whale! So there!'
says Poppinlock, triumphant. Lomu parries:
'Bet you a Jag you can't describe a whale!'
'Whales are what it rains when the spinks have gathered.'
That seems to settle it, but Lomu's adamant:
'Sheer 4-Star exhaust! Time we took a vote.
Hands up if you're here or if you're not.'
This is the test of tests for Poppinlock.
He scratches out a minute while he thinks about it.
'Let's consult the bones...' (It's Susan
coming through. We hold our breath.) 'How many
finger-joints make one man's hand?' she murmurs.
'Flim-flam!' Jasta's ash-sprig voice – it crackles,
'You can count me out! Lay off my bones!
I'm sick to death of being fumbled with.
Just mind your own Any Other Business!'
'The ring of truth,' we whispered as he faded,
'the fob-watch of authority at last!'
No one took the minutes or the seconds,
but the meeting was acknowledged as a great success.

CHAPTER IX

In which various aspects of creation, procreation and recreation are considered.

The New Adam

Lischka shaved her head. 'Sisters,
it is up to us to recreate the earth,
kick-off Sunday, first light, sharp,
and this time on a democratic basis.
We shall invent one perfect male to start with.'

Thus Adam was created out of air so pure,
so utterly untainted and seamless,
that no one could do justice to his qualities
except in negatives. Adam just is flawless.
We are currently inventing his language
which will be unbelievably inoffensive.

The Visitations

So many births this season! We're all pleased.
It's like an epidemic, or – as Xencha puts it –
'It never rains at all but it pours whales.'
She overstates: there are a lot of spinks
(also, sadly, stillbirths and Siamese owls).

Down in the plains they get wind of the news
and send a grey suit up to register the births:
'Get on with it, I don't have time to waste.
All the details – fathers' names first.'
We shuffle guiltily like innocents.

'A sort of something in the air, perhaps?'
'Otherwise, a sudden rush of wind?'
'Nonsense!' (Ezreq, curt): 'We make our best
out of sheer sweat and labour pains.'
'I see,' he smirks, 'Immaculate conceptions...'

Poppinlock: 'I found mine in the murmurings.'
The Registrar goes purple: 'Something of a tomboy
are we, sissy?' But our Lischka knows their language:
'We found them all under a gooseberry bush.
The rest came airmail via a swan or goose.'

We're lost in admiration, but the grey suit isn't:
'In other words, your brats are illegitimate!'
Poppinlock asks what it means. (He hasn't thrown off
polysyllables as yet, and still breaks out in spots.)
'It means, in common language, that your lot are BASTARDS!

And don't think we don't know about your habits –
orgies, rubber goods, porn shops, transvestites,
whips, French maids with lisps, the stench of Sodom!
You can't even tell a man from a woman!'
We nod as one (wo)man. It's a problem.

Sexy Frolics in Mistila

The local inhabitants of the picturesque village of Hum, which nestles in the foothills of the Mistila range, are enraged and incensed by what are described as 'sexual orgies' up on the plateau at nights. It is reported by a casual observer that nude women habitually appear, not only in the backstreets of Hum, but also in his guesthouse bedroom. Asked why he failed to apprehend them, he replied: 'They're slippery bitches, sneaky, like all their kind.'

The Mayor of Hum, who wishes to remain anonymous, reports a sighting, through binoculars, of five or more, 'coupling like rabbits'. Local shopkeeper and Defence Warden, Mrs L., says: 'We are disgusted. These so-called people don't even seem to eat. None of them has ever once entered my shop. And if they tried I'd have the dogs on them. They're animals. All they ever think of is sex.'

The Regional Chief of Police reserves his comment, thereby adding fuel to the smoke.

Ex-Colonel Pippinghast, Councillor and local landowner, remarks: 'We need to smoke them out before they breed. The nude boys are the worst.'

A sighting committee, fully armed with binoculars and rifles, has been set up under the command of a local Magistrate. (*Editor's Note:* Mistila has been earmarked as a holiday resort.)

A Perfect Match

Dear Father Superior, Do not believe
the salivations of the Press. The good souls of Mistila
are attached remarkably, I almost said religiously,
to the institution of marriage. They do it again and again.

No, don't misunderstand. Monogamy
is, in their phrase, 'the only serious way to play'.
The bond is neither carnal love, nor rank, nor property,
but what Crampfold terms the Principle of Mutual Astonishment,

which has to be demonstrated once a year.
Folk converge from miles off for 'a good match'. Nor
are they mere spectators, for they hoot and jeer
at predictable gestures. Infidelity is slow-hand-clapped.

At the least hint of collusion the match
is declared null and void. Some couples play safe:
long silence punctuated by a few non-sequiturs, much
like marriage elsewhere. In the olden days, I am told,

weddings were truly gladiatorial affairs.
Fatalities were not unknown. One famous bride-to-be
staged the spectacular illusion of a funeral pyre where-
in she hurled herself to inflame her beau's cooling ardour

with pre-emptive suttee. Duly stupefied,
he leaped into the flames she had spoken out of air;
he tripped on a boulder, cracked his head and died.
'But beautifully,' the old ones shake their heads and sigh.

The re-match I witnessed was tame
by these standards. *He* brought a ripple from the crowd
with his juggling with starfish, blindfold. All the same
her Maori oaths seemed a trifle studied. At the end

something more seemed called for. I
stepped forward, sprinkling from my little phial
of holy water. The crowd erupted, lifting us head high,
the three of us, and declared us most astonishingly wed.

I have tried to explain my vows.
They slap their thighs and roll about and cry 'Too much!
The game is over!' What am I supposed to do? And how?
Father, I stand in mortal need of your advice.

Delete As Inapplicable

Father Goodheart has asked me to thank you
for your request/communication with regard to
baptism/marriage/adultery/funeral rites/sodomy
which he has read with concern/interest/delight.
Unfortunately, due to unavoidable absence,
Father Goodheart is unable to be of assistance
in this immediate instance but wishes me to enclose
our standard leaflets for your guidance, *viz:*
Baptism and the Flesh; Matrimony and the Flesh;
Adultery, Sodomy, the Flesh and the Devil;
Flesh to Ashes and Dust to God, and *Fleshpots.*
We trust that you will find the answer to your
query/statement/confession in one or more of the booklets.
Meanwhile, Father Goodheart has enjoined me to express
his joy/condolences/concern with regard to whichever
birth, marriage, bereavement or trespass you have kindly
informed him of. I am also instructed to thank you
for your donation/forthcoming donation/bequest
to the Missionary Fund/Christmas Party/Church Roof,
and to reassure you that, as ever, the Lord is with you
so that no prayers shall be left unanswered.
Indeed I should like to take this opportunity
to inform you that our Ansafone Confessional
is due to be operational in the not-too-distant future,
and that it is newly equipped with updated data
on penances for every possible infringement
(with Credit Card facilities). All clients
have a chance to win a cruise for two (plus).
We hope that you too will take advantage
of our *Super-Sin-Win Phone-In.* (Judge to be announced.)

58

Adam's First Words

'In the beginning was the Woman
and the Woman was God and Her Word is God,
and the man is of the Woman, not the Woman of the man
(as I guess St Pauline must have said, on top of which
I'd like to add that *she* would not have shaved her head
or let herself be shorn by sexist pigs).
I myself am flawless and a feminist.
Who could do justice to my qualities?
I am, indeed, the Woman's handiwork,
therefore, in honour of my Maker,
I worship and adore Myself.'

('I'm only human; everybody makes mistakes,'
says Lischka in embarrassment, 'The program's bugged.
Shall we delete him now or wait
to see if he develops into someone else?'
A bleep from Adam: 'Me-Me-Me...'
'Not that *again*,' groans Lischka, 'Quick, delete!'

Alys and the Oral Tradition III

The barber-surgeon snaps his bag shut – 'Operate?
Ten months, you say? Nothing but wind in there.
Or maybe water. Not my speciality, at any rate.
Expect my bill. Good night.' – as Maxwell bumbles
in his wake. The door bangs. Alys winces. She turns
her face to the open window, her lips moving. *Come
lift me up, love, pour me out. Oh, don't be long.*

CHAPTER X

In which we bask in success and the bright light of publicity casts certain shadows.

Fame

The phone rings (cordless) – somebody for Ezreq
from *The Echo*. She's renowned.
They want to send an aircraft to transport her
to the plains for an appearance on *That's Life*
(fat fee and fat expenses paid).
Poppinlock's excited: 'We'll have TV
and a Jag before we know it!'
(He's gone off polysyllables of late.)
The problem is that Ezreq can't be found.
Lischka says she saw her last at bluelight
in her dirty overalls – a grey smudge
trudging up the donkey-track with pick
and shovel and a little backpack,
slipping on the scree and staying put.
'She ought to be put down,' says Poppinlock,
'Look, I can take ten steps to each of hers.'
The words trip from his lips. He's sharp,
we all admit, *and* his clothes become him.
Ezreq would be lumpen on TV. Those overalls!
Who on earth would see the sounds she makes?
So it's agreed that Poppinlock should go instead
and put in an appearance on his own behalf.
Ezreq reappears for an instant and we tell her this
apologetically. She cuts us dead.

Post Zamonism
An excerpt from the introduction to The New Wave, *Fabel & Windrush*

Beyond Jasta, beyond Ezreq and even beyond the Zamonist Move-
ment (until recently known as 'La Nouvelle Vague') an entire new
era opens with the work of Poppinlock. Whereas the work of Zamon
and his followers is insubstantial to the point of invisibility and in-
audibility, Poppinlock discards the mere meaninglessness of mean-
ing in favour of multiple metaphors of no-meaning which actually
appear, in the fullness of their dissolution. We need only compare
his 'Double-Double Negative' with any of Zamon's untitled pieces
to make our point:

> No news is no Jag in the flatulence of no-life
> on *That's No Life* on no TV set.
> No father in no corridor of no air
> sniffs no wind like no cough.
> No door is not locked when no one
> "stays put" or exits in or out.
> No fingers finick nothing in the no-light
> which is not unshadowed by the no way back.

What is so extraordinarily new here is the reappearance of the word
"like", reminding us of the Jastan epoch. In this context we should
also note the words "stays put" with their hint of wistful undertones
and echoes "contained", so to speak, within quotation marks, and
so gathering entirely new non-meanings via the irony they suggest.
Although Poppinlock has been scorned by the disseminators of the
cult of Zamon (notably on *That's Life*), we see him as an innovator
of the first order.

Gifts

'Xencha, are you sad?'
Another night like an Ice Age
tightened round us. We were only faces.
In the caves of the fire

were flying fish,
a snake-pit and a looted tomb,
a doll's house in a furnace, crowds fleeing,
and whatever Xencha saw.

Those always-startled eyes...
I wanted to protect her, painfully.
'No,' she said slowly, 'But you are giving me
a sadness. Why?'

Then I knew. 'At home
I have children. Two. As we planned.
They are tall and fair.' The bright vault
crumbled and flared.

'As we planned. And yet
there is the other. In a dream
that comes, there is a third I always
almost recognise.

She is dark and small
and never speaks and watches me
with such eyes I can't touch her or begin
to explain. And every time

before I wake it's she
who gives me something, a glass, maybe,
of clear water or a smile that's half a question.
But I think you know.

When I find my way home,
Xencha, will you come? We could give
you, give you back, so much: clothes, toys,
such food...' She frowned,

'This *giving back*...
You wish to cancel out the gifts?
And if you could, what then? You will find
yourself with nothing.'

Browsing in the slag
next day I found a nugget with a grey-
silver dust in its crystals. 'Xencha,' I thought.
She glanced once, then

screamed and flung it
far out of sight. 'That one is wild.
It cannot be tamed. Though your people try.
Never tell!' It was the first

time I saw Xencha cry.
'Never tell them. Never let them come
for it!' 'What is it?' 'We say *ashes-before-fire*.
You say *uranium*.'

A Naming
Report from Dr Crampfold

As you know, I am renowned for having
catalogued child-naming ceremonies
in the eight acknowledged corners of the globe,
in service stations on the motorways
and in the heartlands of amusement arcades –
but in *this* case there seemed to be no child!
Preliminaries took the usual form
and guests assembled, each one with a gift
(although, as usual, in their case,
the gifts had neither weight nor size nor shape).
This time, the old one, Ul'ma, officiated.
'Now is the time to name the name,' she said.
'Whose is the child? And where is it?' I asked.
'Hush! This is religious,' Xencha whispered.
Ul'ma took the gifts and retired into a recess.
Days passed. (Was it days or weeks or months?
They have no time, no calendars, no clocks.)

Eventually, either before or after,
Ul'ma stepped out in the full regalia
of her naming dress, and raised her arms
and waited for the shuffling to cease.
('This will be the moment of the naming,' Xencha hissed.)
It was. 'I name her Breeze-Block,' Ul'ma pronounced.
Everybody clapped. It was just perfect,
they all agreed. Corks popped throughout the night.

I was not satisfied. 'Where is the child?' I persisted.
'We're naming names, stupid,' Xencha answered.
I adapted instantly, as is my wont, and asked:
'Who are the parents of the name, then? Tell me that!'
She shrugged: 'Most likely *Block* was Ezreq's gift,
and *Breeze* was mine – or maybe someone else's.
Ul'ma will abandon it in any case.'
'What happens to your...orphans, then?' I ventured.
'We murder all our darlings,' she replied.
(But here I would ask you to suspend your judgement
pending my investigations. Xencha's answer
may be just a herring. Nothing's as it seems.)

The Murders

We were surrounded by a cordon of police
in uniform. They hid behind the goats:
'Okay now, come out quietly with your hands up.'

They made us stand against a rock and frisked us.
'Anything you say may be used in evidence.'
Dr Crampfold made polite enquiries.

It seems we stood accused of many murders.
Until the guilty party had been given up
into the arms of justice all of us were suspects.

Of course we all admitted our own guilt
but said that Ezreq was the murderer *par excellence*.
They handcuffed her, but Lomu was enraged:

'How can she murder if her hands are tied?'
Their Chief said he should learn to keep his trap shut
so as not to complicate a clear-cut case.

And then they asked us, each in confidence,
how Ezreq had disposed of the remains.
They seemed quite interested. We were thrilled.

Lischka said, bluntly, that she'd borne a living child
but Ezreq had pronounced it stillborn,
hacked it up and chucked it down a mine.

Susan added that she'd seen a lot of bones,
especially her father's, underground.
'Who said that?' the Chief snapped, 'Stop murmuring!'

Still, all of us agreed it was Ezreq's fault.
She'd exterminated Grandmas, Grandads, babies,
mothers, brothers, sisters, cousins, uncles, aunts:

'A job's a job; now *do* it, and to hell with sentiments!'
She's always right, but still it always hurts.
We wept over the names of our deceased but listed them:

'Jasta', 'Sonny', 'Mummy', 'Your eyes', 'Nan',
'Our President', 'Those eyes again' and so on.
When she got back, she buried them again.

CHAPTER XI

In which a silence is broken, and others fall.

A Crack

It all happened in a blink. There
was the Other One, staring at his rock.
The usual silence. Then a bellow. Poppinlock
toddled off, as if to his next appointment,

having spotted the flaw, the hair-
line fault, and tapped. It was enough.
He blew its locked vault in a little puff
of dust. The Other One raged. Only Xencha

dared to take his hand. Then he wept.
She led him back to us, to Jasta's place,
no longer Other, simply One. His monsters played
in the firelight. Some of them were wise.

Bruntiminy went to Lomu. We all
saw the justice of that, except Lomu: 'What
the schist *is* it?' 'You must untie that knot,'
said One, 'or it will be your undoing.'

The *grazzle* used to rage somewhat
but was vegetarian. The hopeless *morbulents*
laid down a ground bass to our old laments.
But One frowned: 'This is no time for sports.

Through that crack I saw the Wee
Equal Empsy Square. Men are building it.
Nowhere is safe. The stone on which you sit
can be undone. Trust no one, not even me.'

What More Could You Want?

Where are the crowds? The girls around his kidney-shaped lagoon
aren't quite the newest wave. On an ever more crackly line

the Cigarillo Man pours oil on his troubles: 'Sic transit,
kid. Relax. A few years, you'll be ripe for the cabaret circuit.'

He's got a bijou hacienda. Honorary PhDs. All the highs
you can buy. A place in the history books. And STAR IN SKY-

JACK DRAMA DASH: headlines. It was last year's top disaster
(now a major film). Some nut demanding home rule for some nowhere.

I have a device. Full of powers. (It may have been a Walkman.)
Will blow you to the winds. In fog, fuel on the red, the 747

circled some nonexistent airstrip. Deadlock. Then a new demand:
No psycho-shit! I will speak with Zamon. He will understand.

Zamon didn't hesitate: 'Lomu? Never heard of the guy! Mistila?
No such place. From my fairy tale period. Juvenilia.

Like the Brontës' Gondal. (Now he's established, he refers
amply to the Pittsburgh Companion to the English Literatures.)

You know, Charlene and Emmy-Lou. I'm into real things now,
like angsts and zeitgeists and which famous friend fucks who.'

Why has he triple-glazed his windows? He imagines whispering
campaigns against him. Most nights, he's kept awake by murmurings

he takes for the fault-line flexing, ready for the Big One.
He will invest in new foundations. He calls the builders in.

He fires them. It's the sight of their overalls. And why
should the sound of a concrete mixer make a grown man cry?

Wind from the hills. He shivers. The slick pool blurs
blue to grey. He stares into the ripples. One white feather

twitches and rides towards him. All at once it comes clear,
his final, finest work, using all of him: how all his air

like unstrung pearls might glitter out and, rising, grow
towards the surface as the myths say souls might, going home.

Post Zamon

He's stale news already. Lischka
brought the headlines: FALLING STAR
IN LAST PLUNGE. Ezreq was gone, where

no one knew, out for the annual cull.
She had stooped to a pool. A trickle-fall
of peat-brown water chirred. She saw

how bubbles slapped down by the force
danced back against it as if to retrace
their way to, and beyond, the source.

CHAPTER XII

In which there are violations, but the rule of law asserts itself.

The Last Act

1 *One*

If anyone, he was the one
to part the clouds and lead us through.
The day the wire came down

we raised a cheer. But he
knew better. *They* were coming *in*. Alone
he walked into the jaws of a JCB.

'Whatever you would do
to my land you must first do to me,'
he said. The men downed tools

till the police came.
'Nowhere is safe,' he said. 'What earthly use
is your *caution?*' His name

appeared on the charge as One,
Of Many. 'Guilty? Innocent? It's all the same,'
he told the jury, 'But when

will you find yourselves?'
To the judge: 'The very stones will be undone.
How will you guard your cells?'

There was trouble in the air,
crowds gathering from nowhere, speaking in fables,
writing them. They called it Scripture.

At a word they would have swept
the courthouse aside. Too late, One saw the danger.
'Eat my words!' he wept.

The few who heard
rushed off to found a sect, eating words and wine.
        Just then a siren sneered.

        The judge washed his hands
as the Specials burst in. The crowd scattered
        in the path of their armoured van.

2 *The Chief of Police's Hangover*

'You don' wanna talk to me...' Six bottles of grog:
he was the only survivor. 'She's gone, y'know. You didn't?
Come to this, has it now? Not even worth a good rumour?
All talking about *him*, are they? Siddown friend 'n' listen.

She got cured. True fact! Two years confined to her bed
then...Yes, it was *him*. Friend o' yours? You gotta admit,
he's weird. Under armed guard, he was, too. Just a glimpse
out the window...Am I glad? Am I grateful? Am I, shit!

At least I had her.' He clapped me on the shoulder
several times. 'Fine woman, my wife. Was. Oh, Alys...'
He blubbered. 'Oh, my little goose.' He took another
swig. 'The bitch. Up and left. To follow *him*, of course.

Where? There you have me, friend. No one tells me anything.
You're talking to a man of no account, didn't you know?
A nobody of consequence. I'd have liked a kid. Leave him
my medal. Now I'll never. Besides, it's only brass. No,

I don't know where they took him. I'm no use to you.
But if you find him, say...Oh, say I'm sorry.
This whole damned thing's a pig. But siddown, look,
here's another bottle. Won't you talk to me?'

3 *Signs*

        We were left with signs and symbols.
They tore the topsoil. They laid black rubber cables

thick as truncheons. We heard him cry.
They switched on the juice. We saw him arch and writhe.

The piledriver thudded all night, blow
by (never when you next expect it) blow. Ul'ma came home

stricken. She'd tracked from Ministry
to Ministry, miles of corridors. None of them had any

One on their files. Secret Police?
they said. That's just a fable. From the old régime.

If they *seemed* to exist
that was only the shadow cast by guilty consciences.

You wish to file a complaint?
('Clever sods,' said Poppinlock, 'That's *our* game!')

We watched concrete like cold gruel
slopped into pits. Xencha began to cry. So we knew.

Only Lischka was there
when they led him out into a little empty square.

She sells them the red flowers
that mark the condemned man's heart. Don't blame her.

How else would we have heard?
Tell them: You are all now, were his last words,

I was only ever One.

The Bailiff's Tale

Of course they chose *me* to evict that lot.
I was "dispensable" and "upwardly immobile"
but I showed them. Bastards! They got my goat,
apart from which they'd paid no rent for years –
if ever. (Typically, all the files were lost.)

I had a job to do and I did it, yes *Sir*, right?
The place was earmarked as a holiday retreat,
permission had been granted, there'd be motels,
discos, artificial ski slopes, solariums,
jacuzzis, pleasure steamers and the lot,
right down to dirigibles and whales
and atmospherics – ghost trips down the mines,
echo-chambers, massage-parlours, skeletons.

The first motels were creeping up the slope
already when I reached the base by chair-lift.
From then on it was just a mist of sweat and footbite.
God knows how long it took to reach my target,
but I got there finally and stopped
to catch my breath and shave behind a rock,
then stepped out briskly, briefcase first.
But here's the odd part – I found no one, nothing,
not even a ramshackle hut. I suspect
they'd done a moonlight. Not a bean was left,
not even a footprint or a dirty bit of wax.
The light up there is spooky though. I don't quite...

That was ten years back. I got early retirement
due to tinnitus – not bells and such, just
murmurings inside my ears at nights,
and sometimes words, although they make no sense:
"flapjack", "sprag" (or "spraggle"), "skink"!
My analyst – a Mr Poppinlock – suggests
another trip up there might do the trick
but it hasn't been developed yet. Some legal hitch.
Some Zamonson appeared with trumped-up deeds
to prove that the estate is his. It seems
he's a direct descendant (illegitimate)
of somebody of substance (presumed dead).
Zamonson's got the jargon right so can't be faulted
but no case is airtight, and it's rumoured
that our President-For-Life is interested in the site.
Uranium, lad, that's where the future lies.
But keep it to yourself, right? Buy shares.

Ezreq's Bluff

It was Scriptural like David and Goliath:
the bulldozer on one side *versus* Ezreq
in overalls, arms folded.
'I shall not budge,' she stated.

Sam went berserk: 'Christ! Not another
bloody pinko Greenpeace bitch!
Shift her or I'll flatten her!' he shouted.
And then he slumped over the brake and wept.

The foreman climbed up: 'Easy, Sam.
We all see things. It's just the air. It's twisted.
That's why we get danger-money, lad.
I swear blind it's a fact. Now ram that rock!'

Ezreq stood her ground. Sam stared
until his eyes cleared and he saw the light.
The bulldozer advanced and in its wake
the fog folded like a testament.

The Last Sight of Xencha

'What's a story when there's no one left to listen?'
She tosses the question into a mossy adit
like a stone. 'I am,'

says a voice. She peers in. At the fringes of light
sits a man of no colour; hair, beard, skin,
even his eyes are white.

'Uncle! I thought I'd made you up. So you're true!'
Far below, yellow excavators flense the hill.
The wan man nods, 'And you?

Go back. Make them a doll-child. Smile. Down there
those eyes of yours will serve you well,
whereas here...' She stares

into the dark a long time, then 'Uncle? Can you sing?
Do you dance? No? Then I'll teach you. Wait,'
she bobs back, 'One more thing.'

By a rusty stream, she fills her tin bowl to the brim.
She leaves her reflection in it.
Then she follows him.

You Are Invited

The Director and Management of Star Uranium Inc.
request the pleasure of your company
to visit and inspect their Mistila site.
Why not bring the family? Enjoy a day out
in breathtaking scenery by air-conditioned coach.
No need for cameras. We must insist
you take advantage of our unconditional FREE GIFT –
twenty panoramic views in Supa-Kolascoop
of all the vistas all of us have dreamed about.
See everything you'd like to see – not just
the foothills of the Lischka Range,
but even Ullman Copse and Lomu's Leap!
Take in Ezreq's Bluff and Zamon Falls!
Hear the "mystery" of Alys Springs explained.
See the film behind the cartoon characters
of *Grumpy Grampfold's Dreamtime Favourites!*

The coach is fully fitted out with videos
and all facilities. Our hostesses
will serve a range of local specialities
from *Chèvre-au-Gratin* to Maxiburgers
(accompanied by *Cloudberry Nouveau*, of course).
Good old-fashioned spirits on the house!
You will not need to exit. See the lifelike
crocodiles and pterodactyls
by the kidney-shaped lagoon of Inlock Creek!
Laugh at Jasta's Death Mask from the comfort of your seat.
Marvel at the Xencha Stone, in 4-D Panascape
and view a scaled-down model of our Plant.
Hear Grumpy Grampfold's *Folklore-into-Progress*
on a no-expenses-spared, commissioned tape.

Remember that your future is our business.
Our safety record has been framed and mounted,
so Zingalong with Star Uranium Inc.
Look out for us. We're coming your way sooner than you think.

EPILOGUE

In which terminal uncertainties afflict an old man, and us all.

Hereafter

lemme set the seen. year twenty twenty. this is now.
in the One Big City (where else is there?). see me come
to the chekout of my Block. Security givs me the snout.
"where yu goin grandad?"

                              "nowhere Sir" (humble-humble)
"oversixties disco." he aint tunin in. his palm is out.
i coff a hundred. private enterprise.

                              / WE INTERRUPT
YOUR THOUGHTS TO REMIND YOU THIS PROGRAM COMES TO YOU
THANKS TO MAILD FIST PROTEXIONS. FIST COMES FIRST! HERES
LOOKIN AFTER YOU! /

                              chekt out. i fade down the blackstreets.
head for the shanties. clear the britelites of the Blocks
(private utilities) quick as a switch. im in powercut country.

/ THIS IS A NEWSFLASH. SLITE UNREST IN UNOFFICIAL QUARTERS
OF THE CITY UNDER CONTROL. STAY IN YUR BLOCKS. STAY TOOND!
(switch off, yu hear gunfire most nites) /

                              im too old to care.
i stand out like a gold tooth among stumps and fillins.
when the punk militia shows (plf? fnlp? whos spellin?)
i say "doc Pop". one jerks his kalashnikov, "over there".

                              *

place must of bin a fillin station once. that old smell.
brings back...there are slum bums all over. the forecourt
is docs waitin room.

they shuffle mutter cringe aside
a path for me. great guz, i think, its come to this.
but the good doc takes what comes. he cheks me inside.
doctor p.p.inlock.

what sorta shocks you
bout the doc aint just his acute shortage of size
(dwarves are two a fiver in the slums) or his oldworld
way of talkin or his moonybald head or his icecube eyes
but...is he old or young? babyface. wrinkled hands.
still it comes natural to call him Pop.

'No!' Pop snaps his fingers, 'Short attention span.
It's getting worse. Try to concentrate.'

"somethings faulty
in my tunin. i got interference. different stories breakin in.
like someone hashd my scrip."

'Commercial breaks?'

'not that,'
i sez, 'worse. like, there's no message.'

'Could be memory,'
he sez, 'There are pills you can take.'

"but is it real?
is it, like, official? i get dreams. a car. not an armourd car.

79

a car just to go in. anywhere. i lost it. dreams. but they feel
like true..."

        he pulls me up a crate. he knocks the last
jag of glass out the window. 'Watch. It's a screen,' he sez,
'Tell me everything you see.'

                        "...the usual beggars goin past.
old dumb juan. some dosser in a wreckt Ford. and a whore
in the square. now shes faded. theres why. an armourd car.
police. chekin out the walls. posters. some popstars megatour
rippt in half. eviction notices. a sprayjob: LIBERTY OR.
think its a bloodstain. brickwork. theres a little girl. shes
got a stone. the police. shes goin to...no! shes seen me.
shes...doc, its happenin again, doc. its those eyes...

  im sorry..." his arm is round my shoulder.
  i cant see for tears. "guz knows ive tried.
  ive tried to understand. doc, is it too late?
  what does it mean?" he rockt me. very gently.

'Once upon a time, there was a savage tribe
who danced for rain. Danced, maybe days, maybe
weeks. Some fell exhausted. In the end, what joy,

the rains! Now, *we* know that it always rains
there, every week or two. Always has, always will.

But could it be they just *liked* dancing?'